Finding Your Divine Purpose

Finding Your Divine Purpose

**YOUR GUIDE TO LIVING AN EMPOWERED,
FULFILLING, AND ABUNDANT LIFE**

Dennis R. Chamberland

© 2017 Dennis R. Chamberland
All rights reserved.

Cover Photo by Rico Mandel

ISBN: 0692893768
ISBN 13: 9780692893760
Library of Congress Control Number: 2017903825
Higher Purpose Publishing, Laguna Niguel, CA

To my dearest Shirley: thank you for the invitation!

Love bears all things.
Believes all things.
Endures all things.
Love never ends.

Contents

My Daily Prayer · xiii

Prologue · xv

Introduction · xxi

THE IMPORTANCE OF TAKING INVENTORY

Chapter 1   Know Where You Are, Know Where You're Going · · · · 3

Chapter 2   Let Failure Strengthen You · 7

Chapter 3   Beware of Society's False Image of Perfection! · · · · · · 11

Chapter 4   Faith and Religion · 15

SCUTTLING THE SHIPS

Chapter 5	Harnessing the Power of Belief	21
Chapter 6	Overcoming Fear, Doubt, and Worry	31
Chapter 7	Embrace Change—Don't Fear It	35
Chapter 8	Where Is Your "Intersection of Excellence"?	41

IT'S NOT ALL ABOUT YOU

Chapter 9	Living a Life Free of Judgment	47
Chapter 10	The Money–Happiness Connection	53
Chapter 11	Living a Life of Abundance—There's Enough for All of Us	55

TAKING PERSONAL RESPONSIBILITY

Chapter 12	Words Can Be Lethal Weapons or Powerful Expressions of Love	61
Chapter 13	The Four Decisions	65
Chapter 14	Your Pet Knows the Truth	69

REALIZING INNER ALIGNMENT

Chapter 15 Receive and Give, and Expect Nothing in Return··· 73

Chapter 16 Tuning In to Messages Intended *Just for You* ······ 77

Chapter 17 The Universe Will Conform around
Your Best Efforts and Intentions···················· 83

Chapter 18 The Importance of Loving and Accepting
Yourself First ···································· 87

Notes ·· 93

My Daily Prayer

Dear God, thank you for one more day. Thank you for walking with me and opening my heart to love. I love you, God, my Angels and Guides and I ask that you be with me today, watch over me, protect me, and keep me safe. Help me to easily welcome abundance into my life. Clean me, cleanse me, and clear me of all negative spirits, attachments, energies, and thoughts, allowing only those spirits, attachments, energies, and thoughts with the highest of intentions and for my highest good to connect with me. Thank you, God, for all the blessings you've allowed me to receive and for all the blessings I continue to receive. I am truly grateful and appreciative. Thank you, God.

Prologue

Growing up in a small town where everybody knew everybody else was a big challenge for me. My parents sacrificed so they could send me and my sister to the best private schools, alongside all the kids whose families were very wealthy and influential. My father was an amazing man, a barber by trade, and my mom worked tirelessly during the days and evenings to take care of us kids. As a family, we were just able to make ends meet; we weren't wealthy by any measure.

As I look back at my life as a young kid, I realize that, at my core, I was a very sensitive, thoughtful, caring, and compassionate person. But being like that made me too vulnerable; to survive, I buried all that stuff way down deep so I could become the person I thought I needed to be for my friends to accept me as an equal—or at least so they wouldn't perceive me as the inferior person I thought (on so many levels) I was.

Early on in my life, I started to believe that being *me* wasn't good enough. How could the son of a barber match up to the other kids whose parents were either major casino bosses, well-known celebrities, or mega-resort owners? So there it began. I started creating a facade to make myself feel better and more on par with the other kids. My best recollection of the smoke-and-mirrors masterpiece I had created was the lie that my dad was a business owner who owned many apartment buildings and small strip malls. It wasn't true, but it did make me feel better about myself. It made me feel that I was just as accomplished as those other kids I hung out with. It was common for me to feel embarrassed about my dad when he would show up as himself because he wasn't showing up as the person I had built him up to be; I had put him in a no-win scenario, and he didn't even know it.

As I grew up, I became even more insecure about myself; I was truly lost. I would mimic the behavior of my cool friends, dress like my cool friends, make gestures like my cool friends—the list of dysfunctional behaviors was almost endless. I remember that the stress of going out with my friends at night was so intense because I was constantly on guard and playing a role, making sure I fit in and didn't stand out—because standing out meant (in my eyes) that my secret sense of inferiority would be exposed, and I'd be revealed as a fraud.

Throughout my early teens, I had so much judgment about myself that I also began to judge others—I was not a very kind person. And when I went to college at a private university that lots of my childhood friends also attended, I became even more materialistic. My goal at the time was to graduate and get a job making *lots of money*, because that was what I thought success was all about. Right out of college, I was the youngest person ever hired in a San Diego–based brokerage firm. During my four years with the firm, I was consistently one of the top-five-producing associates, and I made lots of money, but I was miserable. So I decided I would leave the brokerage industry and begin building high-end homes with the intention of flipping them for a profit. My innermost belief that I was not good enough followed me even through early adulthood and into business. I was *extremely* motivated, but I was riddled with insecurities that led me to make deals that were not in my best interest.

The next two years or so went very well, and I was beginning to realize some success when, in the midnineties, the housing market evaporated virtually overnight. I was caught flat-footed; I had two newly built homes on the market that I had dreamed would sell for big money. Well, that didn't happen, and after liquidating my properties, I found myself essentially penniless within a period of four months.

I was oblivious to what was really happening to me at the time, but essentially, God had stepped in to provide a life-changing lesson for me.

God stripped me of all my material possessions. I was forced to sell all those material things that I had used to define my sense of self-worth. As I look back at those subsequent two years of hardship, I can say they were the most challenging and revealing times of my entire life. I was blessed to have a friend who allowed me to rent out a room in his house (even though I had no money to pay him); otherwise, I would have been on the streets. I had no car, even though my father had bought me two beat-up old trucks so I would have transportation. But because I needed money, I had to sell them both. I remember I would gather loose change every day and find just enough so I could go to the Burger King down the hill and eat lunch. I worked at a resort driving a limo, and I would go in, even on my days off, so I could eat a meal and wouldn't go hungry that day. I remember that one day after a very long shift, I was so tired I doubted I could make the long, four-mile walk up the hill back to my room, so I "borrowed" one of the limos for the night so I could drive home. The next morning, they reported the limo stolen about twenty minutes before I drove it back into the motor pool the first thing the next morning. I lost my job because of that—boy, was I screwed!

Months later, I remember walking up that long, steep hill one night—all alone, crying as I walked—and asking God why I had to endure this cruel existence. Right then, the reason why became crystal clear. God's answer was that he had stripped me to my core so I could rediscover myself and what was really important…and what was clearly not important. God's message to me was that I was not a reflection of my material possessions but instead a powerful reflection of his divine spirit. My conversation with God and my commitment to him and myself was that I would live a good life and be a good person, one who felt love, acceptance, compassion, and kindness toward myself and others.

That next morning, my whole world began to change, and my "spiral of lack" began evolving into a blessing of new paths and opportunities for healing and growth. Realizing on a fundamental level that I was my own roadblock, I consciously sought to keep my life as simple and straightforward as possible; I understood that in the past, I had tended to create maze upon maze of complexity, smoke and mirrors, a lifestyle that was simply unsustainable.

FINDING YOUR DIVINE PURPOSE

In my adulthood, all the way up to my early forties, I had become what I call "accidentally aware," meaning that over time, I was able to gather enough unconnected pieces of the "consciousness puzzle" to live a relatively aware, accidentally conscious life. Then, one day, the woman I was dating (who later became my cherished wife) invited me to join her for a weeklong personal-growth workshop in Las Vegas that was hosted by a well-known personal-growth life coach. This would prove to be a life-changing week for me.

Fast-forward to the current day: I am free to be me without really caring whether others like or approve of what I'm doing or saying or how I'm being. Ah, such a good feeling! I do my best to treat people in a kind and thoughtful manner, without judgment and without preformulated conceptions. I consciously choose my friends as well as who I no longer want to be friends with. Those who add value to my life are cherished and loved and a meaningful part of my life, while others who don't resonate with me and my life path, beliefs, and outlooks are no longer receiving any of my energy, even though I wish them well in their lives without me. I am truly blessed.

Introduction

The story you've just read is true. It's the story of my life, and I suspect that it may bear many similarities to your life's journey too. To this day, I'm still in awe at how many people tell me they've struggled with the same issues. That realization is what led me to author this guide to living an empowered, fulfilling, and abundant life. I'm honored to place it before you, and I hope it provides you with the empowering tools and insights that will change your life just as they did mine.

I was in my midtwenties when I realized how unhappy I was and that I needed to make some serious changes if I was going to find happiness. I knew it was going to be of critical importance that I take inventory of myself so I could get a solid grip on who I was and where I was in my life. For me this was a much-needed first step, because I had been so successful at filling my life with layer upon layer of lies to bolster up my low self-esteem that I had no idea who I really was.

I was raised in a fairly strict Catholic household. I went to a Catholic elementary school, high school, and college. Growing up I went to church every Sunday—there was no other option. As I grew into adulthood, I felt more and more disconnected to my Catholic faith and eventually stopped going to church on Sundays. While I remained very spiritual, I realized that I had grounded my faith within the confines of an earthly religion rather than grounding my faith in the divine spirituality of God—learning the difference was a huge breakthrough for me.

My personal-growth journey wasn't an easy one. I knew that growth required doing things differently, and it meant pain and discomfort as I created an entirely "new normal" for myself. Frankly, there were at least several instances when I retreated back into old habits and beliefs instead of plowing forward in the face of painful change. I persisted, though, and ultimately made a decision to block my path of retreat, what I call "scuttling the ships," which is a naval term used to describe the process of making a ship useless—typically by sinking it. This was a turning point in my life; it represents the period of time when I made my greatest self-discoveries.

One day, years ago now, I was walking down a hallway at work when I said hello to a colleague who proceeded to pass me by without even looking at me or saying a word. I didn't really even know this guy, but I was so angry that he could be so rude as to not even acknowledge me that I thought, "What the hell did I do to him?" I can remember talking to others in the office that day about my encounter in the hallway, describing what had occurred and making uncomplimentary comments about the individual who had perpetrated this affront upon me. Only later that same week did I discover that the colleague I had vilified earlier had received news of the passing of his father, and when I saw him in the hallway, he had been on his way out the door to be with his family. As I reflected upon that moment, I realized that his actions had absolutely nothing to do with me, yet I had chosen to judge him and his actions and to create a whole story around his silence—I chose to take things personally and make it all about me.

Soon after that, I realized that I needed to make conscious decisions about the things I said and the things I did. I needed to align my thoughts, words, and actions to reflect the good inside of me and to create good outside of me. I realized that I could choose what I wanted to create and that my thoughts and the words I used to express my thoughts were key to my taking personal responsibility for what I created in my life.

It had always been easy for me to give, but it was so very stressful for me to receive. For so long, I believed I didn't deserve to simply receive without giving something in return. It turns out that I had misunderstood the whole concept of giving and receiving. Once I realized that giving and receiving were both a part of a circular, energetic flow instead of being separate linear actions, I was able to receive graciously and realize that joy comes to the giver as well as the receiver. Additionally, I began to understand that when my thoughts, words, and actions were in alignment with who I am and with what nourishes me, I was taking inspired actions—I was living within my divine purpose.

Before you begin reading, I ask one thing from you. I ask that you suspend what you think you know and be open to learning new things you may not know. I ask that you remove all preconceived notions and opinions and remain open to the possibility of embracing a new path, a new way of thinking and feeling about yourself and others.

The Importance of Taking Inventory

CHAPTER 1

Know Where You Are, Know Where You're Going

For me, understanding where I was in life enabled me to gain a better understanding of God's plan for me—it was the crucial first step. For you, it is important that you have persistent faith that you will realize your dreams and aspirations regardless of your current circumstances, and at the same time you must be brutally honest with yourself about the facts of your current reality. Never waiver in your belief that you will ultimately succeed.

During the Vietnam War, Admiral James Stockdale was shot down and imprisoned in the "Hanoi Hilton" for almost eight years. How did he survive during his time as a POW as he watched many of his brothers die? Admiral Stockdale concluded that to survive, one must retain faith that one will prevail in the end, regardless of the difficulties one is currently experiencing. Admiral Stockdale's view was different from simple "optimism" because it required embracing the brutal reality of your current situation—where you are at any point in your life.

Faith that is grounded in a hard-core reality check fends off the disappointment and devastation that comes when you are only optimistic, because it keeps your expectations grounded in the reality of where you are and not the fantasy of where you wish you were.

In order to get to where you want to go, you must know where you are; otherwise, you wander aimlessly without direction. If you received a map and were shown your destination, but you did not know where you were starting from (your starting point), then the map would be useless because you would be lost and directionless. In the same way, embracing the brutal reality of your current situation is critical to moving forward. Understanding where you are will enable you to begin your journey based on truth, which will allow you to live a life of joy and abundance within your divine purpose.

By truly knowing where we are, we are then able to accurately begin to understand where we want to be and what we must do to get there.

An exercise I regularly do at least once a year is to write down an assessment of my current life situation at that exact moment, as well as the current state of my business. Then I write down my revised personal and business goals using the same criteria. The difference between where I am and where I want to be represents my "journey" toward realizing what I want.

Remember that this exercise is only as effective as you are honest with yourself. This is no time for inaccurate thinking. The more honest and "to the core" you are, the clearer your path toward your ultimate goals will be...and the easier it will be for God and the universe to align to support you in powerful ways.

CHAPTER 2

Let Failure Strengthen You

Part of knowing who you are and where you're going is understanding how your failures are a key part of your overall growth and your path to future successes. Stepping into new territory, both personally and professionally, can be pretty scary stuff, and there will be times when you succeed as well as times when you are less than successful. I recall my own personal experience with a business failure that had a devastating effect on me. In the midnineties, I started up a home-building company—I built high-end spec housing with the intent of selling homes for a profit.

As an entrepreneur, I took some big, yet calculated risks. Even though I made sure everything that was under my control was controlled and working smoothly, the fact is, I had no control over the prevailing economic environment. By the late nineties, the banking industry was in a free-falling implosion; savings-and-loan companies were closing in record numbers. Despite my best efforts, I was forced to liquidate two finished home projects at a *major* loss. Needless to say, this devastated me—I had never failed at anything before, and suddenly I had become the thing I feared the most: a failure. For years I was crippled by the soul-crushing thought that I was a failure. I just wasn't able to get past it, until one day I realized that many, if not most, entrepreneurs have to deal with failure before they realize success.

This helped me understand that with each disappointment comes the gift of growth and wisdom. To learn from our failures or mistakes and to grow from them is truly a gift from God, because only by experiencing the darkest sadness can we appreciate the brightest joy. Only by living through the most terrible of failures are we truly able to appreciate the most resounding of successes. Only by suffering heartbreak are we truly able to experience real love!

We must get up and shake ourselves off during those difficult times, or we are choosing to be less than we are truly meant to be. Realizing our divine purpose is a journey of personal growth and awareness that requires persistence and commitment to living today, not reliving yesterday.

Within each failure lies a gift of awareness and wisdom. Meeting failure when we were expecting perfection can lead to personal devastation; failure can become a wound that never heals as long as the expectation of perfection remains. But we are not perfect. All we can expect of ourselves is our best effort, and at the end of the day, whether we succeed or fail, we can hold our heads high, knowing we did our absolute best.

Few failures in our lives are more demoralizing than failing in business, failing ourselves, or failing at love and relationships. Accurate thinking on these three areas will make all the difference between whether you get yourself up and dust yourself off or live in the energy of shame, guilt, and blame.

Failures in Business

In your business or professional life, there will be setbacks, but don't let the disappointment of failure make you fearful of getting back in the saddle. Successful people do what unsuccessful people won't—they don't let failure be the way the story ends. Remember that each failure brings you one step closer to amazing success.

Failures with Yourself

Know who you are, and stop trying to be someone you're not. You are perfectly unique, and you are a full and complete creation of God. Truly believe that you are good enough and that you deserve all the blessings God has for you. Value yourself enough to believe that you deserve happiness, love, and joy. Love yourself as you are, so that others can do the same. Expect that you'll put your best effort into each day but don't expect perfection.

Failures in Love and Relationships

Love and accept yourself for who you are; then you won't need to seek approval from your partner. Know that what you put out is what you receive in return—so be the partner you want in your life. Losing yourself in a relationship only hurts you. When you give up yourself to make others happy you are the one left unhappy, depleted and unfulfilled. Love yourself first, and that energy will attract others who will easily love you just as much as you love yourself.

CHAPTER 3

Beware of Society's False Image of Perfection!

Taking inventory of your life is not a journey of self-judgment that welcomes shame, guilt, and blame; instead, it is a journey toward freedom and truth. Everything that exists is a creation of the one living being—God. Everything is God. God is love, and behind all the insulating layers we create, there is pure love, pure light. We are limitless beings that are directly connected to God and the universe; we are one being, and not separate from the other.

As children, the filter of society does not cloud our vision, but as we grow, we begin to experience the harshness and cruelty that come with nonconformity. We've all heard it said that "kids can be so cruel," but where did they learn this cruelty? They've learned to judge others who are different from what is expected. Being a good boy or a good girl means that you behave and listen to the guidance and instruction of your teachers, your parents, or your guardians. But what are their qualifications? Who taught them?

From our earliest ability to learn, we have learned from others who were taught by others, from generation to generation. Each generation accepts the social norms of the previous until we are expected to act, think, and be a certain way…but that is all a massive lie.

With each new day in our lives, doing what is expected brings one more day of acceptance, one more day of not being judged by others. It is the fear of being judged and of not being accepted that keeps us walking on the treadmill of society's expectations.

The more we walk on this path of societal expectations, the larger the gap grows between who we are and who we are pretending to be based on what society expects of us—until one day we wake up wondering who we are and why we are so unhappy.

At its core, the life society creates for us is a lie. Finding the truth is what will set us free. The truth brings freedom from the fear, doubt, and worry that fill the life of someone who lives to meet the expectations established by others—established by society's false image of perfection.

The truth frees us from the judgment we receive from others and allows us to live a life where the judgment of others does not affect us; if we do not judge ourselves, the power of judgment from someone else does not affect us.

Everything we believe about the world and ourselves, all the concepts and programming we have in our minds, and all the confusion and clutter that have built up over the course of our lives are because we've been believers in society's false image of perfection.

As we begin growing into adulthood, we become more and more assimilated into society's norms and expectations. We are constantly bombarded by commercials, articles, TV shows, and billboards that show us how we are supposed to be and what we are supposed to do if we want to be happy. Eventually, our subconscious begins to agree with these views of what we should be, and we then begin to believe we are not good enough. How can anyone be good enough when compared to society's image of false perfection?

Since society's image of what life should be is only an imaginary life of marketing perfection that no one can attain, we are constantly reminded that we are not good enough because the reality of our lives doesn't match up to this. The end result is that we end up rejecting ourselves because we've come to believe that we are not good enough. This constant judgment we send and receive creates a victim mentality inside of us and fills us with guilt, shame, and blame.

Eventually, society's image of perfection and the rules that accompany this image become a part of the fiber of things we believe in, and these beliefs guide our outlooks, attitudes, and actions. Not only do we judge ourselves when we don't live up to society's expectations, but we also judge others who fail to live up to our understanding of what is expected. You see, when we believe in society's image of perfection, those beliefs become our beliefs, and these falsehoods perpetuate themselves from generation to generation.

The power that judgment has over our lives is *very* strong—so strong, in fact, that it controls our every thought and action. We are so filled with the fear of being judged that we strive for acceptance at every turn. This feeling of acceptance is reassuring and makes us feel good because our actions are enforcing our beliefs.

We are so fearful that we will fail that we don't even try to live our lives in alignment with our divine purpose. We are so filled with doubt about our self-worth. We are frozen, fearful of deviating from what is expected. We are so worried that we will not be good enough and that we will fail so we never take what we believe is too big a risk, one too far outside the box.

At the end of the day, you must love yourself first and remember to replace fear, doubt, and worry with faith in yourself and in the power of God. Equally important is grounding your faith in spirituality and not solely within a specific religion—knowing the difference is very important.

CHAPTER 4

Faith and Religion

OK, folks, it's time to go to that place where passion runs very deep—time to talk about religion and faith. Knowing the difference between the two is key to taking true inventory of the beliefs you choose to welcome into your life.

When I was around thirteen years old, I was having a crisis of faith; as I lay in bed, I found myself talking to God. I was at a point where I was having serious doubts about whether God truly existed. I remember asking God for a sign, a sign that he really does exist. I asked, "If you really do exist, make a car horn honk two times." I lay in my bed in total silence for a couple minutes, and then, out of the silence, a car horn honked two times. From that time on, I have never doubted that God exists and that God plays a critical role in every part of my life.

An interesting side note is that my parents raised me in the Catholic Church. Every Sunday I went to church—it was not an option. I went to Saint Anne's Elementary School, Bishop Gorman

High School, and did my undergraduate studies at the University of San Diego (yes, a Catholic university). By the time I graduated in 1985, I had pretty much earned my stripes as a Catholic. It seemed like soon after I graduated from USD, I stopped going to church. Was it because I no longer felt obligated to go or because I was no longer feeling a connection to the Catholic Church? Fact is my reasons probably had a little to do with both.

As my awareness around the concept of faith and religion increased, I started to realize a clear difference between the two. For me, *God* is the term I use to describe that one Supreme Being, but it soon became apparent to me that others used different names to refer to that same Supreme Being. Whether they used the word *God*, *Allah*, *Spirit*, *Universe*, or something else didn't matter—they were all talking about the same Supreme Being who is the creator and ruler of the universe and the source of all moral authority. In my opinion, all earthly religions worship a God, and while they all differ in the details of how their God came to be, they all hold a deep belief and faith in that same Supreme Being. From the dawn of recorded time, humans have tried to define their spiritual faith and place it in a specific box they call a religion. With the creation of separate religions, there came the inevitable judgment about which religion was the right and most righteous one.

Because humans hold on tight to their religious faith (faith based on their religion), many are actually willing to go to war and die to defend their faith. The issue of religion is a great example of how society creates very specifically defined boxes of conformity, and once humans begin to compare each different box, they begin to judge each box. I struggled with my disconnect between faith and religion for a long time, but I eventually gained absolute clarity on where I stand spiritually. I came to believe that I have a deeply held spiritual belief in that one Supreme Being, the creator and ruler of the universe and the source of all moral authority. After my father passed in July of 2016, I started going back to church on Sundays, but it wasn't for the same reasons as in the past. This time, I made a conscious choice to attend church because I wanted to be open to messages God might have for me. Now I use my presence at church mostly to be in a space where I can be with my inner thoughts and reflections within a spiritual safe space.

No doubt I've grown considerably when it comes to my views on religion and faith. I realized that placing some faith in a religion has allowed me to be a part of a supportive community of good people with, to varying degrees, are spiritually aligned – that said, I am careful not to lose myself in religion. At one point along my journey, I came to know that what my spirituality looked like to me was unique unto me and that it didn't fit within any earthly definition of religion, so I stopped trying to fit a square peg into a round hole. Instead, I gained a clear understanding that my faith was grounded in the belief that there is only one true God that we all share and that the one true God is within me and everyone on earth.

While I am a deeply spiritual person, I also have a strongly held belief that I have the power to create what I choose, and based on my choices I have the power to create my own heaven or my own hell right here on earth. A key piece of this belief is a thing called *Karma*. The Buddhist definition of Karma is, "The sum of a person's actions in this and previous states of existence, viewed as deciding their fate in future existences." In short, Karma is like a massive energetic boomerang that returns all the good and all the bad you do right back to you in abundance. Understanding this, wouldn't you rather have a massive wave of good stuff flow back to you rather then a major shit-storm of bad stuff? Remember that how someone treats me has everything to do with their karma, and how you respond has everything to do with your karma so remember to make more deposits into the karma bank and fewer withdrawals.

Scuttling the Ships

CHAPTER 5

Harnessing the Power of Belief

In AD 1519, during the Spanish conquest of Mexico, Hernán Cortés, the Spanish commander, scuttled his ships and eliminated the path of retreat. This action meant that his men would have to either conquer or die.

This story of the ancient warrior begins when Cortés's men set sail in their eight ships, which were loaded with battle-ready troops. They sailed for months to their field of battle. Upon arriving, the men were met with an overwhelming presence that instilled fear into their hearts, creating doubt and worry that they would not prevail. The captain, in his wisdom, ordered that the ships be burned to the ground. The troops, with nowhere else to go, released their fear, doubt, and worry and committed to engaging the enemy and pursuing ultimate victory—because anything less would have meant certain death.

As you reflect on the story of Cortés and his men, ask yourself if you are *playing to win* or if you are *playing not to lose*. It's fairly safe to say that the men commanded by Cortés were definitely committed to succeeding; otherwise, they would have certainly all perished. As you absorb this, it's important to ask yourself how you are approaching the pursuit of your dreams. Are you taking inspired, persistent action to realize your vision, or are you just dreaming with no action to support it?

Ask yourself, "Am I playing to win, or am I playing not to lose?" I remember as a young kid that I would play not to lose because doing so meant I wouldn't stand out and I could stay in that safe space of anonymity. I would have the biggest dreams that I never manifested into reality because taking action to turn those dreams into reality presented too great a risk of losing or failing. I was that guy in the back of class that most often knew the answer but always let others bask in the glory because I had calculated that speaking-up wasn't worth the risk of being embarrassed or losing credibility in the eyes of my peers. For me being anonymous meant I didn't have to risk being rejected. This pattern persisted all the way through to the end of 6th grade year.

As I entered the 7th grade, I had finally had enough. I was at the point where I was receiving more grief from others then I thought I deserved so it meant big changes and massive realignments were in store for me, my friends, classmates and others in my wider social orbit. That year, at the ripe old age of 12 I must have gotten into no fewer then 12 fist fights with classmates/other school kids and neighborhood kids then I can count. By the time the dust had settled I found myself about a quarter of the way through the school year and now I was the toughest kid in school – not even the eighth graders messed with me. I had reset the paradigm and had found peace. I was respected (most likely feared) by the other kids and was free to the torment visited upon me by others just a year prior.

Interesting thing was that I only took (aggressive) action against other kids when they were perpetrating a wrong against me or in support of those being bullied.

I remember in eighth grade when I, unprompted, jumped into a conflict to defend my good friend Bob from being harassed by a bully named David. Up to this exact moment, Bob had been considered untouchable because everybody believed he knew karate and could kick any body's ass that dared mess with him. That may have been true but I could see that on this particular day, David was about to engage my friend and I couldn't let that happen. Standing by and letting things head-up between those two meant running the risk that Bob would lose the altercation and the balance of power would shift in favor of David and there would be imbalance in the force. Somehow even as a young boy of 13, I energetically knew that balance meant peace and for me feeling was priceless. So I stepped in, took care of business and preserved the balance of power. While Bob and I never talked about what happened on the playground tarmac that day, we both knew what had happened and deepened the respect we held for each other – to this day I still keep in touch with Bob.

What was it that moved me so dramatically from anonymity to prominence within 14 months? Was it luck or was it because I made an absolute commitment—to scuttle the ships, if you will?" Consider this – I decided that I was no longer going to put up with more torment and disrespect then I believed I deserved and decided to go big and take inspired action and become "known". Criticism no longer had a hold on me and I was free (relatively speaking) to create the reality I wanted in my life – I decided I wanted to play to win

Whether you believe you will win or lose, either way you will be correct. The belief that you're the most certain of is the same belief that will lead you to success or failure! Your conviction for *yes* must be stronger than any fear, doubt, or worry that tells you *no*. Remember that where you are *right now* in your life is exactly where you have wanted to be. Whether you realize it or not, your choices have gotten you exactly where you are right now—so if this is not where you want to be, then it's time to start making different choices.

All of those men on Hernán Cortés's ship were products of their environment, and when faced with the life-or-death scenario presented to them by their commander, they chose to fight to survive—in other words, they were 100 percent committed to their success.

On some core level, each of those men embraced positive thoughts, words, and actions to generate positive results. Keep in mind that they would have all perished had they embraced fear, doubt, and worry, since that type of negativity only creates more negativity. Because they were committed to being victorious, they visualized and believed they would be victorious.

Just as we have the power to create the life of our dreams, so too do we have the power to attract people into our lives who will support them or not support them. With that in mind, we should be very conscious about the energy we are creating, because good or bad, we will attract people into our lives who agree with our beliefs, we will attract people into our lives who interpret things in a similar way, and we will attract people into our lives who act in a similar way.

The saying "Misery loves company" is true. Negative people love to gather their flock around them to magnify the impact of their negativity and infect you with their virus. Don't let that happen. Seek out positive energy and abundant thinking while casting out negativity and limited thinking. Don't waste your time and energy hanging around negative people.

Your life dream is unique to you—it's not for you to compare your dream to someone else's dream, and it's not for you to judge your dream as better or worse than anyone else's. Truly believe you love what you do—and truly believe it deep inside of you. It's important to do what you love and love what you do—if either one of these is not present, then you need a change. By committing 100 percent of yourself to what you believe you will give your very best to everything you do, and you will put out the love and respect you want to receive from others.

Remember to *love* people and *use* money. Money should not be the reason for what we do, but it does represent the value we place on our gifts. Money is attached to everything—everyone and everything has a value.

Most people limit themselves because they doubt their own worth and because they don't believe in themselves and their ability to realize success at what they endeavor to do.

Every person is different, and everyone is here on earth for a short time (relative to the eternal lives of our souls and spirits), so we should not waste our energies comparing our passions against the passions of others; doing so only brings back the heaviness of fear, doubt, and worry, and it lowers our spiritual vibration. Why would anyone *choose* to spend one second in that kind of energy when he or she could live within the loving energy of his or her true purpose? It's a no-brainer!

When you pursue your purpose—the reason you are here on earth—you will believe in yourself with the power of conviction and purpose that comes from the divine source of God. Believe that you serve to be successful and that you have infinite power to create what you want.

Making clear choices brings the power of the universe in alignment with your intentions to manifest your thoughts and actions into reality. Your thoughts must be supported by action that is in alignment with what you want to create. This takes conviction and your best effort every day. Your best effort is a full commitment to persisting with faith and conviction every day, knowing that every day will be different from the others.

Do not fall into the trap of comparing one day to the next, lest you invite judgment, which in turn brings with it guilt, shame, and blame. Remember that your best will be different from day to day, but the one thing each day will have in common is that each day represents your best effort.

Hearing people tell you that they're going to put 200 percent into their efforts might sound good on the surface, but when you dig down into what that really means, you begin to understand the depth of judgment, insecurity, and negative energy that surrounds this statement. The fact is that it is impossible to realize anything in excess of 100 percent—since 100 percent represents all there is, it's your best effort. So giving our best effort or receiving the maximum available in any given scenario is 100 percent, and any illusion that we are capable of giving or receiving more than 100 percent is simply a judgment that either our best effort is not enough or that we may have received more than we deserve.

The key to finding inner peace and confidence is this: we must realize that doing our best every day represents our 100 percent effort on that given day and that receiving the abundance of what we want is in 100 percent alignment with what we deserve.

When I think of persistence, I'm reminded of the story of the miner who staked a claim and worked his mine for decades, tirelessly working ten-hour days, seven days a week, with no results to show for all his efforts. One day, the old miner decided he was done. He'd been working for so long with no results that his once-crystal-clear conviction about what he believed to be riches beyond his wildest imaginings had turned into fear, doubt, and worry that he'd been wasting his years in the wrong spot. So without wasting another moment, he put his claim up for sale and was greeted by a young man just getting into the mining business who was very interested in buying the old miner's claim, which was now being sold for pennies on the dollar.

The old miner, glad to be rid of the worthless claim, went on with his life, pursuing other interests, while the young man who had just purchased the claim was preparing for many, many years of hard work with, as the old miner reported, slim chances of ever finding anything. On his very first day in the mine, the young man began to dig. To his amazement, after going just ten feet, he hit a massive vein of gold that, over the next ten years of his life, would turn out to be the largest vein of gold ever discovered in the western United States. Had the old miner just gone ten feet more, this would be the story of his success. But alas, the moral of the story is that you must hang on to the convictions of your beliefs and keep the faith, knowing that with persistence you will be successful and realize your goals. Don't give up when you could be just ten feet from gold!

In the face of adversity, persistence is key as it is the sustained effort necessary to achieve the results you desire. Desire is the energy behind willpower, and willpower is the basis for persistence. Willpower is the ability to focus and control your thinking. To be persistent, you must manage your energy; stays focused on your priorities, and not get distracted by external things.

But how do you receive what you want? Focus on *receiving* what you have envisioned, not on *getting* what you want. The distinction is that one allows the flow of abundance to provide an abundance of what you want, while the other is more like grabbing out of fear of scarcity and is outside the natural flow of the universe.

Receiving of value requires that you give of value. Giving of yourself in a meaningful way to another who will appreciate and value your gifts is a great example of how this principle works. Perhaps you've heard the old saying "Don't throw pearls before swine." The point of this wisdom is that you should give only to individuals or organizations that appreciate and value receiving your gifts; for example, give in instances where giving helps others improve themselves. Give to worthwhile causes, and use good judgment when giving of your time and treasure. Don't give blindly to those who would abuse the gift they have been given, or to those who don't realize they've been given a gift. Give things of value to those who recognize and appreciate the value so that you may graciously receive things of value in return, all the while with no *expectation* of anything in return. Giving in this way releases your energetic grip and allows the universe to generate a greater flow of abundance right back to you.

Another key to receiving what you want is to know your desire. Formulate your desire, and then put a clearly stated desire out to God and let the desire take form. Leave the "how" up to God and the universe. When you give, the universe will bring you what you desire. None of your desires to manifest what you are wanting will appear unless you are ready to receive what you are wanting in abundant supply.

CHAPTER 6

Overcoming Fear, Doubt, and Worry

Removing the energy that fear, doubt, and worry have over how you live your life is key to believing in your ability to succeed, regardless of the obstacles before you. Isn't it funny that we'll put up with as much abuse as we think we deserve? It's true—think about it. The very second we are treated worse than we treat ourselves or are loved by someone less than we love ourselves, we take action to leave that person or to confront that person.

So as you can imagine, the degree to which we will tolerate abuse is directly connected to the amount of guilt, shame, and blame we carry. If we don't love ourselves or we believe we are not worthy of being loved, then we'll attract people who agree with us and treat us accordingly.

One of my favorite authors, Don Miguel Ruiz (author of *The Four Agreements*), says, "The fear of being rejected becomes the fear of not being good enough."

This is so true. In fact, when we are so fearful of not being accepted, we eventually become a person we no longer recognize. I know this from personal experience, because that is what happened to me.

As children, we learn the basic rules of life from our parents, who learned those same rules from their parents and their parents before them. The rules of society are so ingrained that we, as children, don't stand a chance. We are taught that every time we do something "right," we receive a reward, just as when we do something "wrong," we receive the corresponding punishment. After just a short while, we become like trained elephants in a circus, performing as our trainers expect for fear of being disciplined. We develop the need to be accepted and to be loved by others, but we cannot accept and love ourselves.

So every day we live our lives "playing by the rules," fearful of anything that challenges what we've come to believe, because doing things differently makes us feel unsafe. We walk the path of what we know and what we believe. Taking no risks means staying safe.

We accept what we are taught and told, blindly. Even our names and our religions are chosen for us—did you play a role in choosing either of those? Ask yourself, "What other things in my life do I blindly agree with or follow that I truly had no role in choosing?" You'll be surprised what you come up with.

Visualize for a moment a black box. This is where fear, doubt, and worry live. Now visualize a white box; this is where love resides. It's important to give voice to the doubts, fears, and worries we have so that we can rationally address them and reaffirm our true beliefs, which are not based on those doubts, fears, and worries. Don't force the lid shut on the black box, because doing so will cause it to speak even louder. Instead, dialogue with the black box, and reject the false beliefs by confirming that beliefs based on fear, doubt, and worry are inaccurate thinking. Once inaccurate thinking is acknowledged and corrected, energy leaves these beliefs and they fall away, leaving the black box empty.

CHAPTER 7

Embrace Change—Don't Fear It

Change is a constant in all our lives, but releasing the fear, doubt, and worry around change allows you to accept and embrace it. Expansion brings discomfort, and when there is pressure to conform, expansion can also be emotionally painful.

Personal growth and expansion are not easy because it involves change, and change is uncomfortable as you push against your barriers to growth. As you move closer to your goal, you will realize increased pressure, discomfort, and pain that will threaten your love, security, and self-esteem. At that point, a barrier is created and you have a choice to either retreat back to a "safer" place or break through that barrier toward your ultimate goal.

Each time you retreat when facing a barrier to growth and expansion, your progress forward becomes less and less because the barrier contracts with each retreat. Eventually, the pain and discomfort of remaining where you are is greater than the pain of breaking through the barrier, and that is the point you will ultimately decide to break through and achieve your goals. The graphic below (see figure 1) creates a helpful visual of what I've just described:

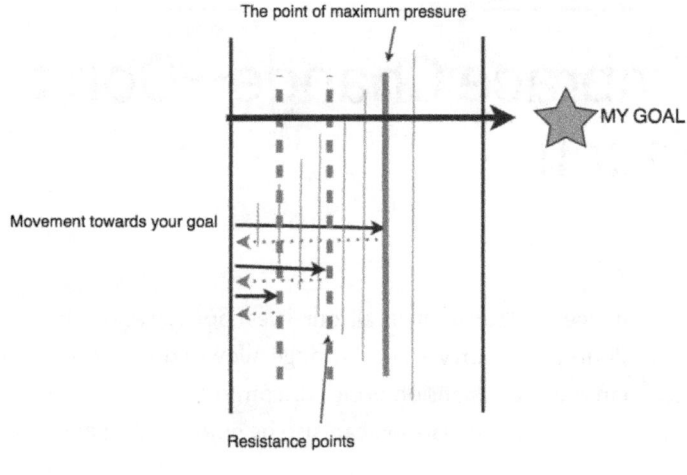

FIGURE 1

Everybody at some point has had a perfect moment in their lives—that moment when all the movement in your life brings you to a point when you find yourself thinking, "I want things to stay just like they are right now," only to realize that perfect moment is shifting into something else. That, my friends, is a great example of change. In reality, change is all around us—it is inevitable because everything is changing and shifting in every way every day, within us and all around us. Nothing stands still—everything is in motion.

The energy of change is reflective, so harness the power of change by being the change you want in yourself—what you put out is what you receive in return.

Through my journey of personal growth and self-awareness, It became clear early on that **I needed to be the change I wanted in my life.** Being the change I wanted involved lots of discovery around what was in harmony with my life purpose and the universal laws. You've heard people say, "you are what you eat" … well the same is true about living a life of joy, peace and abundance in so much as, "we are what we create and welcome into our lives".

Then I decided I needed to **change my personal rules for success.** Early on in my life I made lots of excuses for my lack of success. I doubt I even know what success looked like or felt like. I was so filled with self-doubt that I was nervous (maybe even afraid) to be around successful people because it seemed they could see right through me.

Next, **I started to visualize what success would look like if it were easy.** For someone raised to believe that working hard was the key to success, this was a difficult false-belief to reconcile and cancel out. I threw-out all the old conventional approaches I had previously tried and decided to reverse my field by considering a path of finesse that would produce an elegant solution that would be simple, neat, and efficient.

Thinking beyond common sense was my next move. I knew that a small increase was not what I was seeking – I was ready for big change, big happiness, big success, and big love in my life. So I decided to set myself free and give myself permission to be me and surrender to the universe. I decided to let God be a part of my path forward by following the clues and letting my purpose and desire guide me. **Relying on God and the universe as my source** for all ideas was very important for me and I knew that abundance was all around me, even though I couldn't see it – I just needed the right eyes to show me what was already in front of me.

I knew there would be times when I'd have trouble believing and that fear, doubt and worry would present barriers to my growth, so **I had to remain aware of those times when I was having trouble believing** in my path and purpose and continue moving forward with complete faith and confidence that I would prevail.

Finding a way to keep moving forward made all the difference between just dreaming of my abundance and actually living within abundance. I had to prepare myself to gratefully and graciously receive the gifts that would come and to humbly receive all the abundance within those gifts.

Throughout our lives, we will be faced with growth opportunities that are unavoidable and inevitable. Being grounded in the reality of our current situation will allow us to successfully navigate the journey toward realizing our divine purpose. Being grounded makes us consciously aware of the next steps necessary to move through growth opportunities and closer to our ultimate goal. The diagram below (see figure 2) will help illustrate what this movement and growth process might look like:

FINDING YOUR DIVINE PURPOSE

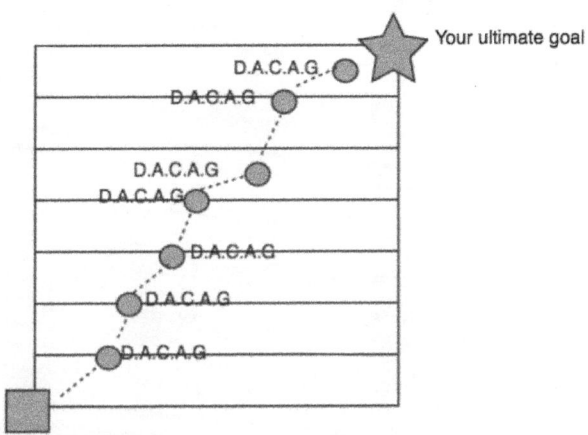

Where you truly are right now

FIGURE 2

D = Decide what you want.
A = Awareness is gained around what is necessary to realize what you're wanting.
C = Change your thinking, attitude, and approach.
A = Awareness is increased around what actions you must take to reach your goal.
G = Growth comes with support from God, your angels, and the universe.

Each time we *decide* what we want, we gain *awareness* and *change* our thinking, attitude, and approach. This brings increased *awareness* combined with *action*, which allows greater clarity of our next steps, resulting in *growth*.

CHAPTER 8

Where Is Your "Intersection of Excellence"?

When I was a young man, I would almost always make my life more complicated by creating many layers between who I was pretending to be and who I really was, each layer creating more distance between me and my truth. But then one day I woke up and discovered I had no idea who I was and why I was here on earth.

So I started using a technique I call the three-circles technique, which an old college professor of mine taught me. It stresses simplicity in its approach, yet it brings massive clarity of purpose. In this first circle reside all the things that you can be your best at. It can include things you are currently doing as well as those things you aspire to do in the future. Remember to differentiate between those things you are awesome at and those you are just good at—doing what you're good at will not make you awesome.

In the second circle reside all those things you are passionate about. Focus on those things or activities that you are truly passionate about—it's not about creating passion in something you are only "so-so" about, but instead it's about rediscovering what makes you passionate. Remember that what you like is different from what you *love* because what you *love* is often in alignment with what you truly want.

In the third circle reside all those things you have always wanted to do or be, but because of fear, doubt, or worry, you have not taken action to realize them. Don't filter your responses here, but instead speak from your heart.

The area where the circles join (see figure 3) is known as your "intersection of excellence"; it's what your passion plan should be based upon. This concept is *not* a goal or strategy to be awesome. It is an understanding of what you can be awesome at! You need to understand that doing what you are good at will only make you good, while focusing solely on what you can do awesomely will make you truly awesome.

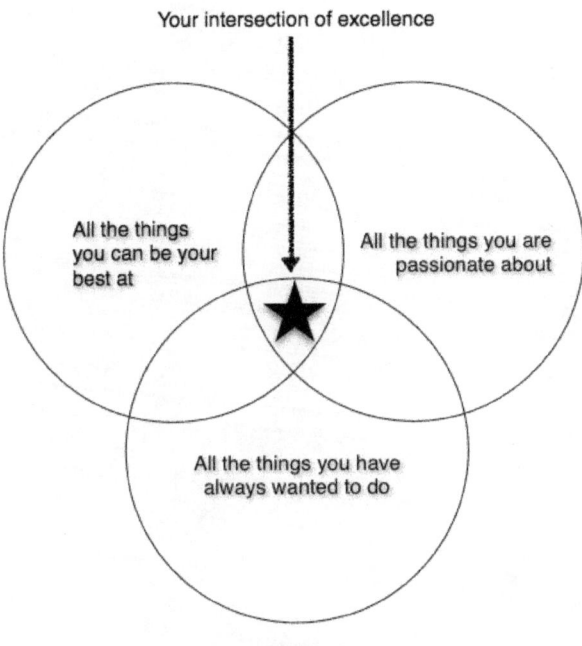

FIGURE 3

It's Not All about You

CHAPTER 9

Living a Life Free of Judgment

Road rage is a fantastic example of how people take things personally and make it all about themselves. Why do we get so upset when someone cuts us off or drives too fast or too slow? Why do we conclude that the person did this against us? Are we so absorbed with self-importance that we think everything is about us?

The fact is that the people who cut us off don't even know us—they don't like or dislike us. So how could they possibly be doing these things against us? Perhaps they were driving fast and cut us off while they were on their way to work. They'd been chronically late for the past week, and with one more tardiness, they would lose their job...so their actions had *everything* to do with them and nothing to do with us.

By taking these types of things personally, we are creating an illusion of negativity where none actually exists—we are creating a judgment that this person did this thing personally to us, that he or she singled *us* out of everybody else on the road—and our response is anger because we don't believe we deserve to be judged so poorly.

People who don't know us can't judge us unless we let them. How can someone be your judge when he or she knows nothing about you? It's not possible—those who judge us without knowing us are instead projecting their own judgments of themselves upon us.

The freedom that comes with the realization that it's not all about us is priceless and life-changing. How can we believe ourselves to be so important that everything that happens to us and around us is all *about* us? The fact is that the life stories of everyone we meet are playing out at those exact moments of connection and interaction. So at the very moment we say hello to that person at the coffee store or buy a sandwich from the lady behind the counter at the deli, our lives and the universe have converged. We are all living in our own worlds.

As you drive to work celebrating the birth of your new child, the person driving next to you might be mourning the loss of her child. As you walk into the bar to celebrate your new job, the person sitting at the table next to you might be grieving the loss of his job.

While you are walking joyfully down the hallway, you might say hello to a complete stranger who is walking down the same hallway in the opposite direction. That person may not respond or even acknowledge you. Does that mean he or she is angry at you or dislikes you in some way? Perhaps that person's reaction has nothing to do with you; perhaps that person just received some very sad news and was on his or her way to the restroom to cry. The fact is there could be many reasons, none of which have anything to do with you, so don't make it all about you. Remember that:

- Other people who don't know us are not taking actions because of us.
- Everyone lives a separate life with a mind and thoughts that are completely different from ours. Others are in their world, pursuing their own views of reality.
- When we make things all about ourselves, we are reverting back to society's false image of perfection, which then requires that we defend our position as "better" or prove ourselves "right" and others "wrong."
- What people do, say, or express is a reflection of their beliefs and values, not a judgment of our beliefs and values.
- All people have their own belief system that is formed from their own life experiences and has nothing to do with our belief system, which is formed from our own life experiences.

Only God can judge us; we are not here on earth to judge. We are here on earth to help each other and to love each other. Where judgment exists, so does the need to make someone right or wrong, good or bad, and so forth. This also applies to how we view ourselves. Because of society's false image of perfection, we are our own most critical judge, and because we judge ourselves so critically, we judge others the same way.

God loves us all equally; we are all uniquely perfect in God's eyes.

The gift that comes with living a life free of judgment is the freedom to be ourselves with no care or concern about what others think of us. We do not judge others, and therefore we do not judge ourselves. Our view is one of a world of different individuals living their lives with love and acceptance for each other. We are not offended by the harsh judgments of others, and we don't feel the need to defend our beliefs or actions because we have no judgment placed upon ourselves. We understand that the judgment coming from others is the judgment they hold within themselves and has nothing to do with us.

Whether someone ridicules us or praises us, it doesn't matter, because we don't need that person's validation. There may be times when we might express ourselves to others, and they might let us know that what we said has hurt them, when in fact it is not what we said that has hurt them—it is their own wounds that our words have touched, those old wounds that have yet to heal.

The result of not allowing ridicule or praise to affect our belief in ourselves is freedom from judgment; we are filled with an awareness and acceptance that everyone is different, and that's OK. When we no longer judge ourselves, we no longer make everything about us, and we are free. We walk with love and without fear of being judged or ridiculed, and we are able to ask for what we need. We can say yes or no—whatever we choose—without guilt or self-judgment because we follow our hearts.

Why do people lie? Is it because they fear the truth is not good enough, or that the truth will expose them as being less than perfect? Either way, a liar lies to himself or herself, and those lies have nothing to do with us—they are simply a reflection of a person's inability to know and see the truth in himself or herself.

Living a life free of judgment about ourselves and others means we don't need to trust in what others do or say, but instead we are able to trust ourselves to make conscious choices. We are not responsible for the choices made by others.

CHAPTER 10

The Money–Happiness Connection

Whether you are poor or wealthy, you need to accept that your choices have led you to your current situation, but you shouldn't take it personally—remember that money is still attracting you, but you are not attracting money. Instead, change your attitude and energy around money, and it will eventually be drawn to you in abundance. The fact is that money has a very powerful energetic frequency around it, and staying in alignment with that energy will affect how much of it flows back to you. It is true that money doesn't buy happiness, but it is equally true that happiness can bring an abundance of wealth and prosperity. The key is knowing what drives what, so that you can create a life where wealth is abundantly present because it aligns with the value you place on your divine gifts.

All human beings exist on a lower-vibrational earthly plane, while God, our angels, and the universe exist on a higher-vibrational spiritual level; the difference between these two vibrational levels is what I call a vibrational gap. Because this vibrational gap is real, earthly beings need to focus on living their lives at a higher-vibrational level, while beings on the spiritual plane make accommodations to lower their vibration to facilitate connection and communication between the earthly and spiritual realms.

Understanding the power of vibration is important to understanding why some people attract wealth while others repel it. Money has a very high vibration, and realizing great wealth requires sustaining a very high level of it. A higher vibration is present where love, joy, acceptance, and alignment, along with an unimpinged connection to God, are present, and a lower vibration exists when these elements are not present. Finding the joy that comes when there is alignment with your divine purpose creates a life of high-vibrational energy, which brings more connection with God, our angels, and the universe and welcomes the flow of wealth relative to the actions you take in support of your divine purpose.

The fact is that money is attached to everything we do and aligns with the value we place on the actions we take in support of our divine purpose. The mistake many people make regarding money is pursuing actions that generate money rather than pursuing actions that bring us joy and that we value greatly. Doing things in alignment with your divine purpose brings happiness, and the value you attach to actions connected to your divine purpose brings prosperity, wealth, and abundance. Essentially, while money is connected to everything we do, it should not be the reason we do what we do.

CHAPTER 11

Living a Life of Abundance—There's Enough for All of Us

The universe wants to support you, but it needs to know your choices. Putting your intention into motion requires that you make a clear choice. The universe does not accommodate for ignorance, and unless you are very clear with what you are wanting, the universe will bring what it best interprets you are wanting.

Everything is spiritually based, and abundance flows from person to person via the divine source, which is God. We own nothing; the universe and God own everything.

Abundance will flow when you focus on *being more* instead of *having more*. Everything we have represents an energetic flow of abundance, which is passed to us through the universe. We must be a living conduit of abundance by allowing its energetic flow to continue flowing on to others, so that the flow will eventually cycle back to us.

With abundance, there is cooperation and not competition. Resist the urge to be competitive in your pursuits. Do not horde. Give freely every day, and choose to follow your path and your truth, because if you don't consciously choose your path, you will unconsciously find yourself in a place you were not wanting to be. It's a conscious choice we must make every day until it becomes automatic.

Anything you don't use or that you abuse you will lose, because the universe will take it from you and give it to someone else who is able and willing to receive it with gratitude and appreciation.

Whatever your divine purpose is, you have to *want it* bad enough to make it happen—to visualize it as if you already have it because the universe has already brought it to you.

By believing in yourself, you don't need approval from anyone else. People will support you for their own reasons—not yours.

Energetically speaking, the left side of our body receives, and the right side of our body gives. An example in practice would be to use your left hand to receive food, money, water, and so on, while using your right hand to provide food, money, water, and so forth, to others. Doing so creates energetic alignment.

Personally, I had lots of problems communicating effectively when I was younger. I was so insecure that I was unable to articulate my thoughts and feelings so by the time I ginned-up the courage to speak, my emotions were so high that situations would often spiral into physical altercations because words didn't seem to be enough. Thankfully, that has all changed and, when faced with a potentially emotionally charged scenario, I ask myself these 4 questions:

- What am I wanting to express?
- What do I want my words to communicate?
- Are my gestures in alignment with what I am wanting to express?
- Are the words I am using in alignment with what I am wanting to communicate?

The big take-away from what I've just described it that *who I was being when I was expressing myself was just as important as what I was actually trying to express* – it was an energetic exchange and not just words.

Words are noise, but vibration never lies. Focusing on a person's energetic expression (vibration) of their words rather than the verbal expression of their words is a more reliable gauge of their intentions and allows you to not only hear the truth, but to feel it too.

Taking Personal Responsibility

CHAPTER 12

Words Can Be Lethal Weapons or Powerful Expressions of Love

The Bible says, "In the beginning was the word, and the word was with God, and the word was God." Words have the power to turn a thought or vision into reality, so it's critically important to remember that words can be an agent for good or evil.

Our thoughts become intentions, which become actions, which lead to creation. At one point, every material thing on earth was once just a thought in someone's mind that, with intention and action, became manifested into reality.

Words are not just symbols on paper or sounds we make; they have immense energy and power to express and communicate creation or destruction, so we must use our words wisely and treat each word with the respect it deserves.

Words can be used to create acceptance and love—but they can also be used to create judgment, fear, doubt, and worry. There are many examples of world leaders who have used the power of words to conquer foes and to enslave nations.

Each spoken word plants seeds within our mind. These seeds take the form of ideas, concepts, or opinions that are used to create or destroy. Our minds are capable of only growing those seeds that we choose to receive. Too often, we unconsciously choose the seeds of fear, doubt, and worry, but we also have the choice to grow those seeds of love and acceptance.

Our words are not only used to create our own reality, but also to influence the reality of others. Words can be used to convince us we are not worthy of abundance, love, and joy—but that is just other people's attempts to use their words to influence our own reality and alter it to fit their own vision of what they think *our* reality should be. This is why we must guard against unconsciously absorbing and accepting the beliefs of others.

We must guard against the opinions of others, only trusting the opinions and beliefs we hold about ourselves. If someone says we are ugly or stupid, we must guard against the acceptance of that belief, because it is not true unless we believe it—and if that happens, then the seeds that have been planted will take root in our minds.

For me as a young boy, I always saw myself as too skinny, and so when anyone would ever comment about my size, it would trigger a strong sense that something was *very* wrong with me. It was not good.

Additionally, throughout my life, people have commented on how beautiful my eyes are, and because I had such a low self-opinion (I wasn't good enough), I did not believe them, and so I grew to hate it when people would comment on my eyes. I wasn't able to accept those seeds of love because I didn't believe I was worthy of love.

Make a commitment to use the power of your words to create truth and love—this is the correct way to use this energy.

Guard yourself against words of gossip or sarcasm, for they are truths wrapped in lies. Self-deprecating humor is a good example of someone who makes light of his or her own self-image and personal view and invites further criticism and poison from the sender.

Do not speak words about people in their absence unless you would speak those exact same words to them in their presence. Gossip is the worst misuse of the power of our words. Gossip is like a powerful virus that can spread from one person to another, releasing its toxic fumes to everyone it comes in contact with.

Using our words to spread truth and love clears societal toxins from our minds and from our personal relationships and creates a shield, protecting us from other's misuse of words toward us. Speaking truth also allows us to reject the seeds of fear, doubt, worry, shame, guilt, and blame and to accept only words of truth and love that have the power to change our entire outlook on life and transform fear into joy and love.

We can measure how well we are harnessing the power of our words by our level of self-love. How much we love ourselves and how we feel about ourselves is directly proportionate to the quality and integrity of our words. When we use our words to create truth and love, we feel great and happy. We feel an inner peace—we are free.

Harnessing the power of our words allows us to be creators of love and frees us from the lower-vibrational energy, where fear, doubt, worry, blame, shame, and guilt reside. The lower purpose must be released in order to gain a higher purpose, and this begins with expressing love for ourselves and showing love for ourselves.

CHAPTER 13

The Four Decisions

Decisions, decisions, decisions...some are easy and straightforward, while others create ethical dilemmas. Whichever path you choose is ultimately up to you, and you are the only one responsible for your decisions. I've created a brief list of four key decisions you'll be faced with every day of your life. Being aware of them will help you consciously navigate them as the choices come to you:

1. Make a commitment (a decision) on your path, and gain awareness of the next steps that appear.
2. Decide to move forward and embrace those new steps, which will then create growth, awareness, and movement toward new possibilities.
3. Decide to embrace faith that everything is going to be OK and that you will prevail.
4. Decide to take action, and continue moving forward through your fears, doubts, and worries.

Most people make the first two decisions on a fairly ongoing basis, but only a small number embrace the third and fourth decisions. Understanding what separates the dream from reality is key to becoming extraordinary—becoming the person you truly are and are truly meant to be.

One thing that blew my mind was the realization that making decisions was not as easy as it once was for me. Because I'd gained a great deal of insight regarding actions and reactions and the implications of each decision I make, it seemed that my choices got much more complicated. So I created the "Dream Diagram" below (see figure 4) to help me visualize what the process of doing things differently (making different decisions) to realize different results looks like.

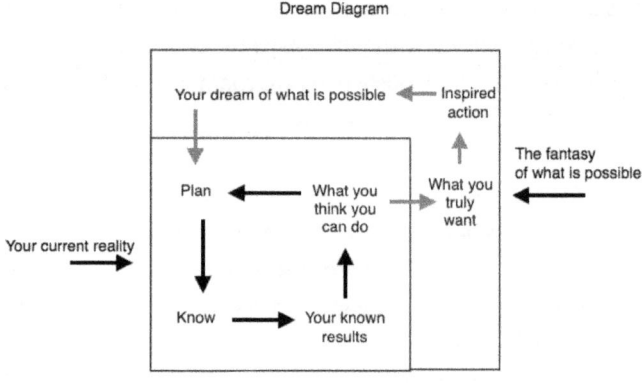

FIGURE 4

The reality you must face is that what you think you *know* is what has gotten you to where you are now—*your present reality*. Based on what you know, you begin developing thoughts of *what you think you can do*, and based on what you think you can do, you formulate a *plan* of action to get there.

The problem with this circular pattern is that it will never get you what you truly want; it will only get you what you think you can have, because it's based on what you know. To break this circular pattern of inaccurate and limited thinking, it is necessary to tap into the fantasy of what you truly want by asking yourself the following: Am I able? Am I willing? In this way, you can discover what you really want, a realization that, with inspired action, will manifest dreams into reality.

The key here is to make the decision to manifest your reality; then you will become aware of the next step in your journey because of a *change in perception* and a different view based on where you are, versus where you were before your decision.

The key to moving through the "Dream Diagram" is the realization that in your mind, you have to want it more than you fear it. In order to turn your fantasy into reality, you have to be willing to do what is necessary.

Dreams come true when you take action to manifest them—then the universe will conform around your clear vision and aligned action to bring you everything you could ever want. You just need to be ready to receive it.

CHAPTER 14

Your Pet Knows the Truth

The only way to take personal responsibility for what you create in your life is to show up as who you truly are. Nobody has that "true you" detector more than your dog or cat. It is true—your beloved pet *does* know the truth about you. Because our furry friends are not crippled by fear, doubt, or worry, they see the truth behind the illusion of reality and the false image of perfection created by society is not there. They see the true you, they see what's in your heart—the love. Our pets are the ultimate confirmation that unconditional love does exist. So if we could only love ourselves the way our dogs love us, anything would be possible.

Many of us are sleepwalking through our lives, never realizing that our daily lives are but a set of routines and habits; we are unconsciously alive. Our current state of being, our station in life, whether we are happy or sad, whether we are wealthy or living in poverty—these are all results of choices we have made.

As we live our lives, it's important to remember that there are no accidents. Everything happens for a reason. This is not to say that our life path is predetermined; instead, I mean we should know that divine timing allows everything to happen for a reason, whether or not that reason shows itself immediately or years down the road. For God and our angels, the earthly concept of "time" has neither relevance nor connection to divine timing. Because this concept of time does not apply within the spirit world, events and actions are able to occur in a beautifully and perfectly orchestrated manner.

The truth is that we have infinite potential. Life and success have no limits, except the limits we place upon ourselves. Think big; the sky is the limit. You know what you want, and you know what to do; you just need to commit to taking action to receive what you want.

It is only after we become conscious of the choices we make, the things we say and do, and the things we believe in that we can live a life of truth that is in alignment with our divine purpose. Only then can we rise into our divine being—our true selves—the reason we are here on earth.

Realizing Inner Alignment

CHAPTER 15

Receive and Give, and Expect Nothing in Return

Giving is an expression of love and brings the gift of joy and alignment for the giver when he or she expects nothing in return. On the other hand, receiving is often an uncomfortable experience for someone who believes they are undeserving of love.

Understanding the significance of receiving graciously is very important. The "energy" behind the word "receive" versus the word "get" is very different. When you are in the act of *receiving* something, you are allowing the natural flow of abundance to come to you, and you are graciously receiving it. When you are in the act of *getting* something, you are actually *taking* something, and when you take rather than receive, the universal flow of abundance becomes out of alignment.

We all have a high side and a low side. Tap into your high side, or your higher/divine purpose. Divine desire comes from the heart—it operates from a place of love and truth. It's important to understand why we are here and to know the following:

- We don't need approval or disapproval from others to do what we do.
- We don't need validation from anyone to pursue and manifest our reality.
- It doesn't matter what others think.

Give up the lower purpose to gain the higher purpose. You can't achieve a higher purpose when you hang on to the lower one.

We've all heard that some people are "givers" while others are "takers." I would suggest that it all comes down to a challenge with receiving. You see, givers give because they aren't comfortable receiving—maybe givers don't believe they're worthy of receiving without giving something in return. But in fact, the giver and the receiver both receive something—they receive love and joy in expressing a genuine gesture to someone else with no expectation of anything in return.

If a giver gives out of fear of receiving, that is not a true expression of love. It is an expression that carries fear, sadness, and resentment. If a receiver receives out of a fear of lack, that is not a true expression of love. It is an expression that carries, fear, insecurity, and a sense that he or she will never have enough.

The universe wants to align to support you in manifesting what you want, but you must create the right environment for the high-vibrational flow of energy to be present.

CHAPTER 16

Tuning In to Messages Intended *Just for You*

All of us humans here on earth have that voice inside us—the voice that helps to keep us aligned with our divine purpose, with the voice of God and our angels. Some of us are so disconnected from our true selves that we no longer hear that voice, or we choose to ignore that voice.

Have you ever done or said something, only to reflect later, "I wish I hadn't said that" or "I knew I shouldn't have done that"? That is affirmation of our voice. I know that in my life, every time I've received guidance from God and my angels and chosen to ignore it, I have ended up wishing I had listened.

We all have the ability to talk to ourselves—to reason things out and to find balanced solutions to the challenges we face. Our minds give us the ability to listen to ourselves. Our voice is our connection to other realms and it allows us to gather and hear information from those other realms.

Our voice often guides us in a way that aligns with our conscious and unconscious beliefs. Over the course of our lives, we gather and agree to abide by many, many beliefs, and over time, some of those beliefs begin to conflict with one another. This conflict occurs when an unconscious belief or agreement conflicts with a conscious belief or agreement. For instance, I grew up in Las Vegas, Nevada. I loved that town because it was all I knew. When I left Las Vegas to attend college in San Diego, I realized just how wonderful it was to be in Southern California, near the Pacific Ocean, in a different climate and environment. For a while I was conflicted, because I had fallen in love with San Diego, yet I had a belief that Las Vegas was my home. Once I reviewed my conflicting beliefs about where "home" was, I was able to consciously create a new belief that San Diego was now my home; I was able to cancel out my previous belief that Las Vegas was my home. Once I did that, the conflicting voices were gone, and there was agreement and clarity.

Because the voice in our mind exists in more than one dimension as well as in God's realm, our minds have the ability to see without eyes and to perceive many realities. Our mind also gives us the ability to believe our voice as well as the earthly opinions of others around us. This gives us the gift of choice.

Clearing and canceling prior beliefs we no longer agree with gives us clarity and allows us to avoid the confusion of many conflicting beliefs speaking in our minds at the same time. It's like a huge conference call where everyone is talking at the same time, and we can't make sense of what is being communicated to us—all those different thoughts and opinions have a different point of view that is being expressed at the same time.

The clarity of a single voice allows us to make conscious choices that are in alignment with what we truly want.

Taking responsibility for your life means being aware that what happens to you is your responsibility—what happens in your life is your choice. Making the choice to create (manifest) your reality will create an intention, which will then create increased awareness around that intention; this awareness will turn into action, creating movement that will turn intention into reality. That movement will be supported by God and the universe in the form of "clues" guiding you along your path.

The key to receiving universal support for your choice of movement is to gain clarity in the following 6 areas:

1. Clarity about what you *really* want—not what you think you should want
2. Clarity about what your passion is
3. Clarity about what brings you joy
4. Clarity about what fulfills you
5. Clarity about what you are meant to do with your life
6. Clarity about what you'd want to do if anything were possible

Focus on remaining conscious of where you need to be to receive what the universe wants to give you—it's already there for you; you just need to see it right in front of you. A change in behavior equals personal and spiritual growth, which leads to a higher state of awareness. Be aware and adapt to the changes in your life.

To gain a higher awareness, truth is necessary. Combining truth with freedom from fear, doubt, and worry provides awareness and freedom from ignorance and false beliefs. A lack of awareness means that you are automatically driven by your subconscious mind, and this state can be a feeding ground for doubt, fear, and worry, which leads to false beliefs.

Understanding the concept of choice requires a deeper understanding of how the four parts of your mind works (see figure 5). First let's talk about the *conscious and the subconscious mind.* The conscious mind allow us to think, accept or reject and make choices whilethe subconscious mind can't do any of those things – it can't even differentiate between what is real and what is imaged. The mind-body can see, hear, smell, taste and touch whilethe nonphysical mind allows us to reason, provides us with memory, perception, will, intuition and imagination.

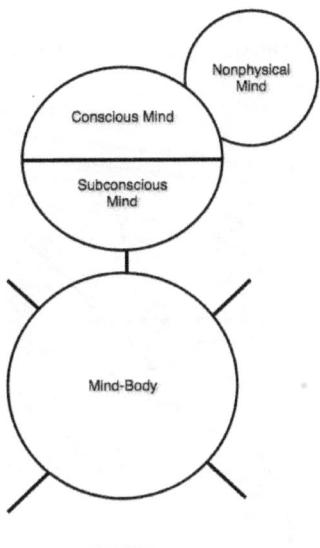

FIGURE 5

When we believe something, our conscious and subconscious minds have reached agreement with reality, which means we become convinced of something. When there is belief, we manifest that belief and attract the universe to turn that belief into reality. We think in pictures. When I say the word "waterfall," our mind automatically generates an image of what we believe a waterfall should look like.

When we face unexpected moments of shock, fear, or negativity, these moments act to short-circuit the inductive filter of the mind and removes our ability to accept or reject a

Belief. When this happens, any belief that enters our mind during moments of shock, fear, or negativity is automatically accepted (see figure 6).

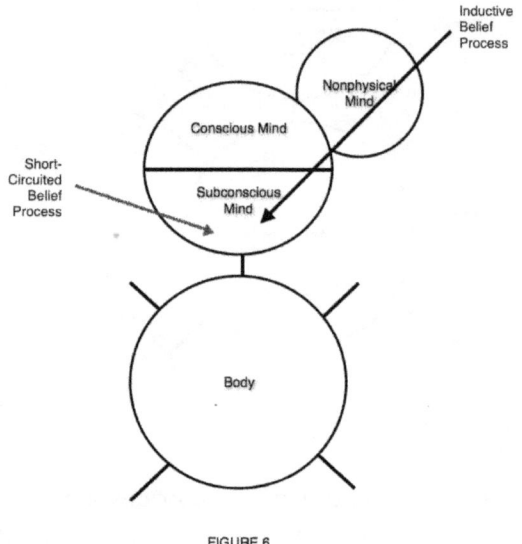

FIGURE 6

Your mind is not your brain; your mind is in every cell of your being. Your mind is part of one universal mind—everything is connected. You are always connected to God and to the universe. You are one entity, not three separate entities. The fact is that the universe is within you, and you are within it—the two are one, not separate. Also, your body and your soul are connected; they are one and do not exist as two separate entities.

CHAPTER 17

The Universe Will Conform around Your Best Efforts and Intentions

The universal laws are in action every day and in every way. They impact everyone equally and make no accommodation for ignorance. What I mean by this is that whether you believe in any particular universal law or not, it still guides what happens around you and within you. For example, if you were to climb to the top of a three-story building and decide to jump off the roof to the ground below, the universal law of gravity would act to bring you crashing to the ground, regardless of your personal beliefs. I've listed eleven universal laws that have been very helpful to me in my journey, and I am hopeful they will be helpful to you as well. Get to know them well, and embrace them as tools to welcome ease and flow into your life.

The Law of Divine Oneness
The law of divine oneness helps us to understand that we live in a world where everything is connected to everything else. Everything we do, say, think, and believe affects others and the universe around us.

The Law of Vibration
This universal law states that everything in the universe moves, vibrates, and travels in circular patterns. The same principles of vibration in the physical world apply to our thoughts, feelings, desires, and will in the etheric (spiritual) world. Every sound, thing, and even thought has its own vibrational frequency unique unto itself.

The Law of Action
The law of action must be applied in order for us to manifest things on earth. Therefore, we must engage in actions that support our thoughts, dreams, emotions, and words.

The Law of Correspondence
This universal law states that the principles or laws of physics that explain the physical world—energy, light, vibration, and motion—have their corresponding principles in the universe. "As above, so below."

The Law of Cause and Effect
This universal law states that nothing happens by chance or outside the universal laws. Every action has a reaction or consequence, and we reap what we sow. This universal law is the law of cause and

effect, which applies to blessings and abundance that are provided for us. The visible effects of our deeds are given to us in gifts, money, inheritances, friendships, and blessings.

The Law of Attraction

This universal law demonstrates how we create the things, events, and people that come into our lives. Our thoughts, feelings, words, and actions produce energies that, in turn, attract like energies: negative energies attract negative energies, and positive energies attract positive energies.

The Law of Polarity

This universal law states that everything is on a continuum and has an opposite. We can suppress and transform undesirable thoughts by concentrating on the opposite pole. It is the law of mental vibrations.

The Law of Perpetual Transmutation of Energy

This universal law states that all persons have within them the power to change the conditions in their lives. Higher vibrations consume and transform lower ones; thus, each of us can change the energies in our lives by understanding the universal laws and applying the principles in such a way as to effect change.

The Law of Relativity

This universal law states that each person will receive a series of problems (tests of initiation) for the purpose of strengthening the light within. We must consider each of these tests to be a challenge and remain connected to our hearts when proceeding to solve the problems. This law also teaches us to compare our problems to others' problems and put everything into its proper perspective. No matter how bad we perceive our situation to be, there is always someone who is in a worse position. It is all relative.

The Law of Rhythm
This universal law states that everything vibrates and moves to certain rhythms. These rhythms establish seasons, cycles, stages of development, and patterns. Each cycle reflects the regularity of God's universe. Masters know how to rise above negative parts of a cycle by never getting too excited or allowing negative things to penetrate their consciousness.

The Law of Gender
This universal law states that everything has its masculine (yang) and feminine (yin) principles, and that these are the basis for all creation. The spiritual initiate must balance the masculine and feminine energies within himself or herself to become a master and a true co-creator with God.

CHAPTER 18

The Importance of Loving and Accepting Yourself First

Yes, *love* is all you need—but a constant dose of gratitude and appreciation is a key ingredient. First, the principle of gratitude keeps you connected and in alignment with your source, with your highest self, with the divine. And second, you cannot be truly happy or live a happy life without it.

Why? Because the opposite of gratitude is resentment. In truth, we create our lives, whether we consciously realize it or not. When we choose resentment, it keeps us in a state of mind where we focus on all the things we don't like and don't want in our lives. The funny thing is that we fail to realize we actually hold all the power in the universe to change anything in our lives. Now, you may be skeptical about your power to create. But what if being in a state of gratitude could bring you closer to your goal?

The power to create also extends to the power to create something good from something bad, especially during those times when you are faced with real adversity, such as the loss of a loved one or the loss of a job. I recall the time when I was fired from a job unexpectedly, and I found myself thinking, "How could this have happened to me?" No doubt I was feeling pretty down in the dumps for several days afterward. Then I decided to shift my thinking and attitude and instead focus on finding the gift that was carefully concealed within the very sad package. What I discovered was the gift of unfettered time with my father, who was battling the final stages of cancer—he passed away three weeks later. The point is that you have the power to choose to be grateful for the setbacks in your life because they present you with the opportunity to search for the lesson, the gift, and the blessing within the experience!

Choosing to be grateful for all the gifts in your life, including the gift of love and acceptance for ourselves and for others, leaves no room for judgment and self-abuse, and it brings a sense of joy into your life that is beyond measure.

Society's false image of perfection and the judgment that surrounds it are the reasons we reject ourselves. They are the reasons why we don't accept ourselves the way we are and why we don't accept others the way they are.

There are thousands of agreements we have made with ourselves over the course of our lives—most of which we did not choose. The most important agreements are the ones we made with ourselves. In these agreements, whether we make them consciously or unconsciously, we tell ourselves who we are, what we feel, what we believe, and how we should behave. This belief system we create is what we call our personality.

Each of us is born with a certain amount of personal power that we build upon or diminish every day based on the choices we make and whether those choices are in alignment with what we truly want. Once you realize that your beliefs influence your choices and that those choices impact your quality of life, then, if you're not loving where your life is, you have the power to make a change by adjusting your beliefs and the choices you make.

To live a life of joy and fulfillment, we must have the courage to consciously choose what we believe and negate those beliefs that no longer represent who we are and what we *truly* believe. By choosing what we believe and by choosing our own personal rules of life, we are reclaiming our personal power.

When someone tells you to fill your cup first, and then you'll be better able to fill the cup of others, do you know what that means? Understanding the concept of the five cups provides helpful insight for remaining in alignment with your true self—your divine purpose. Each cup represents a flow and support for the other—all originating from the first cup of divine source (see figure 7).

- **Cup one** represents God, the divine source of infinite abundance and all that is.
- **Cup two** represents your *being*: who you are, why you are here, and what nurtures you. It is the bowl of the abundant source, which is God.

- **Cup three** represents intentions and feelings. What are your intentions? How do you feel about your intentions?
- **Cup four** represents your vision. What is your vision? What do you see as your future?
- **Cup five** represents naturally inspired action and the manifestation of what you want. Are the actions you take in support of your intentions and vision?

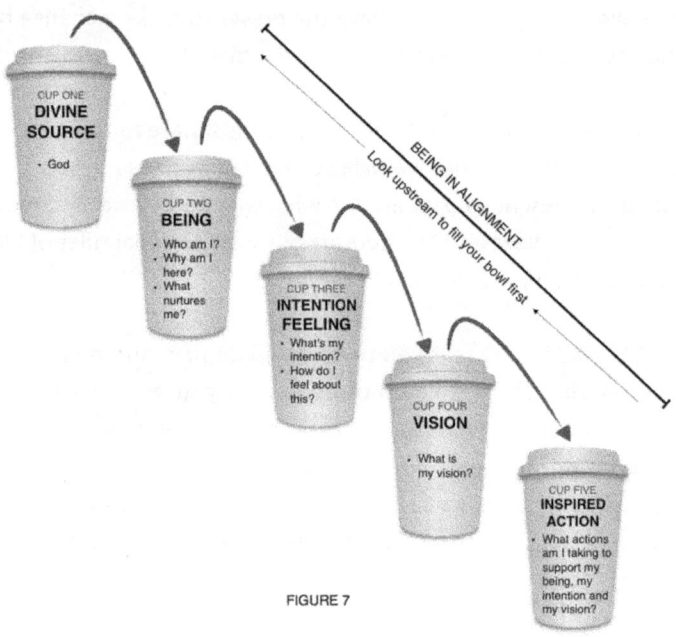

FIGURE 7

When in alignment, each cup feeds into the next from an infinite source of abundance. Taking naturally inspired action based on who you are, why you are here, and what nurtures you (cup one) allows you to draw from an infiinite source of abundance. Taking action based on a vision or feeling that is not in alignment with your true being means that you are not taking action that nurtures and feeds you, which means eventually those cups will be empty because you will no longer be able to continue filling them when your cup is empty. Feed and nurture yourself first, and then you'll be best able to support others based on naturally inspired action.

NOTES

www.ingramcontent.com/pod-product-compliance
Lightning Source LLC
Chambersburg PA
CBHW032006080426
42735CB00007B/519